Headshots
Beautiful Faces of Woman
Adult Coloring Book

By Beth Ingrias

Want to color more for FREE?

Get a FREE 25 page adult coloring book

visit

www.BethIngrias.com

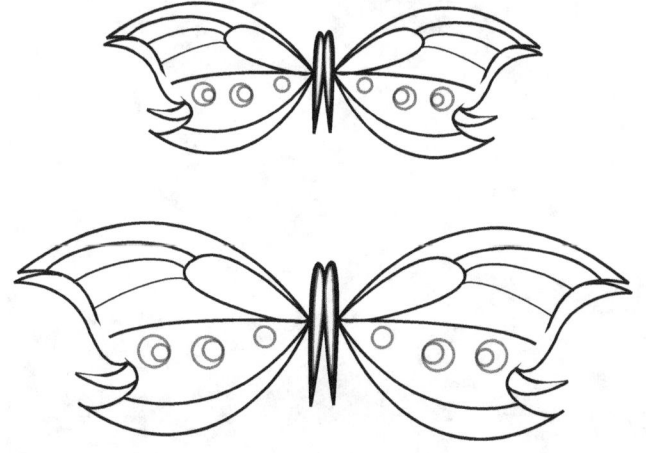

ISBN-13: 978-1-945803-49-9
ISBN-10: 1-945803-49-5

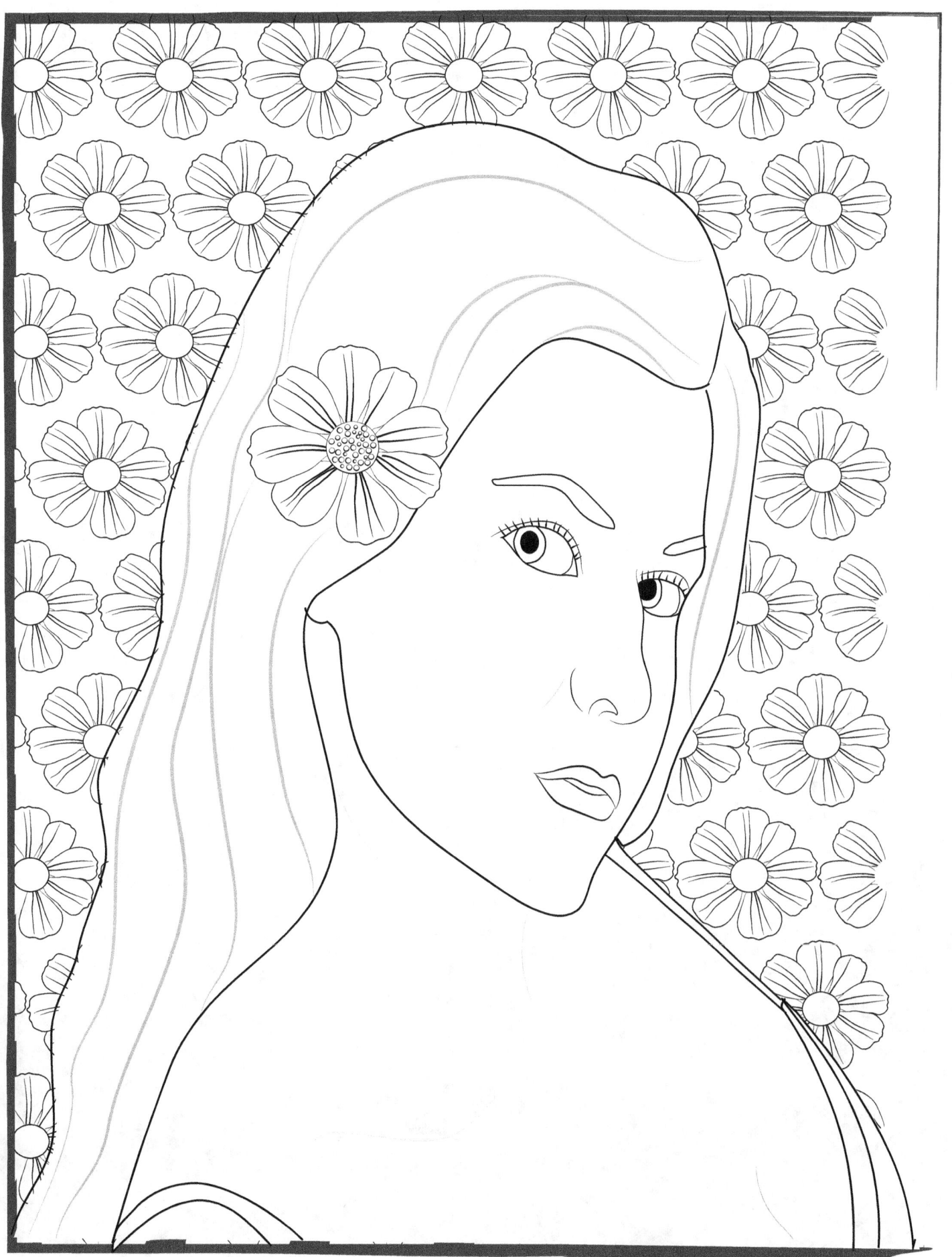

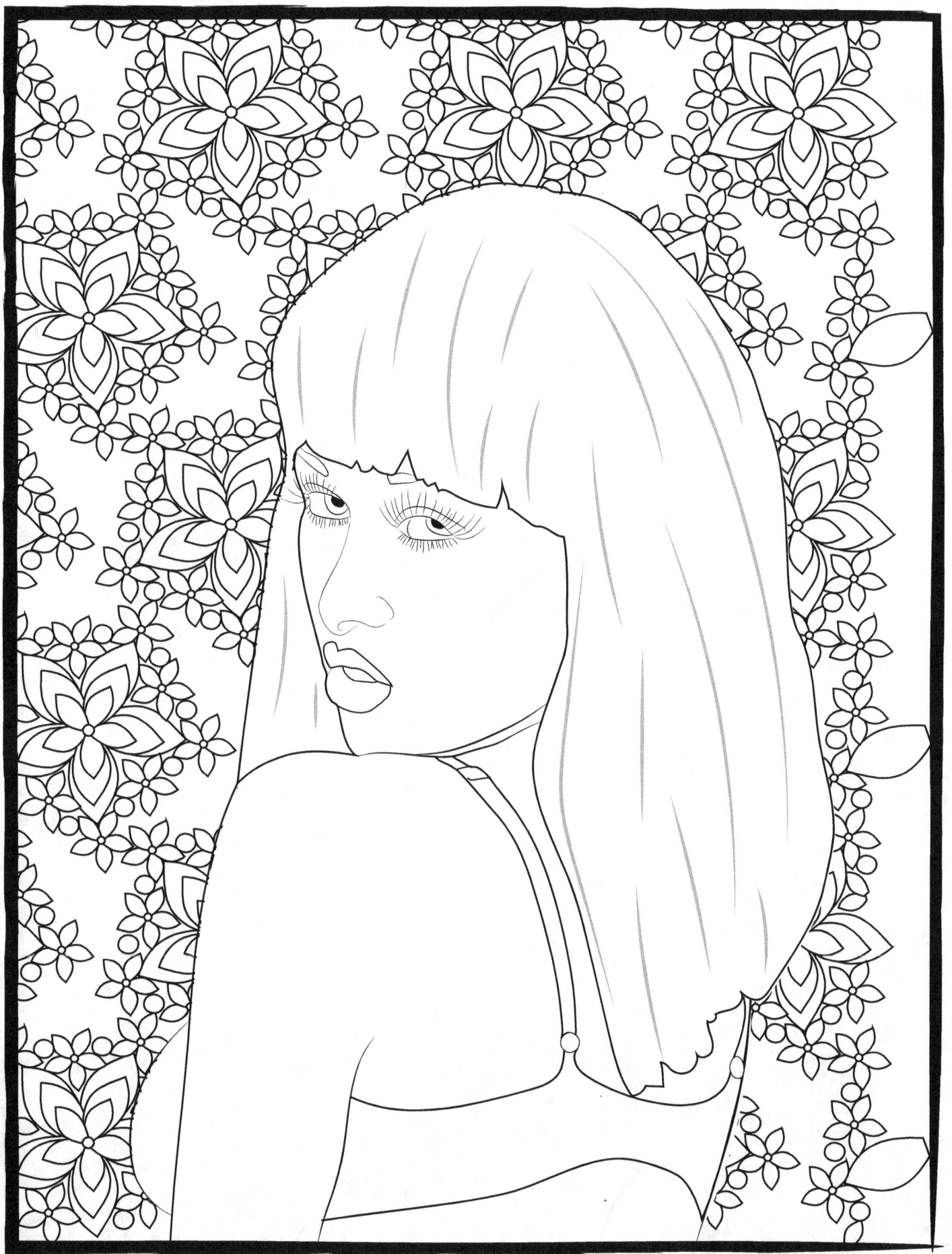

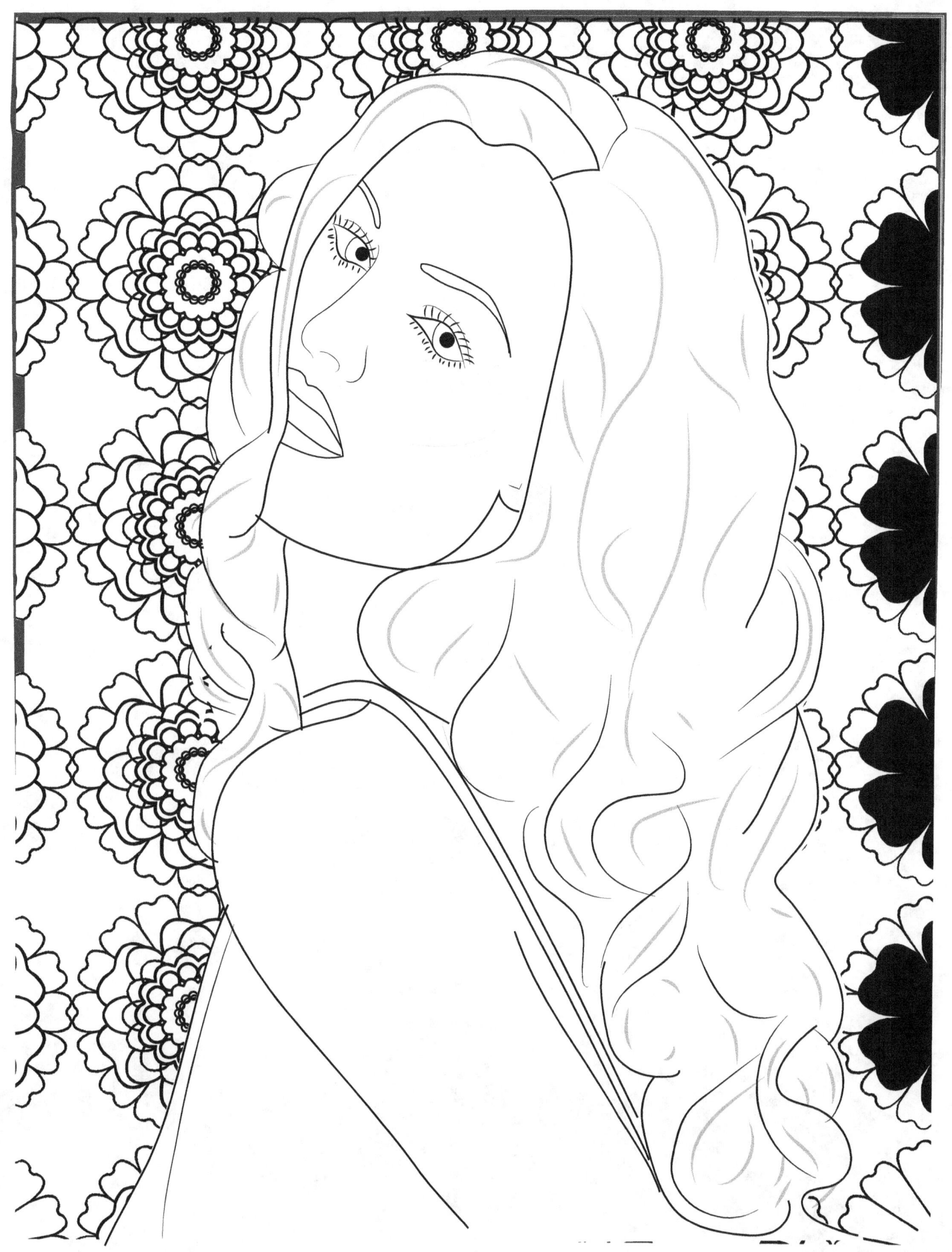

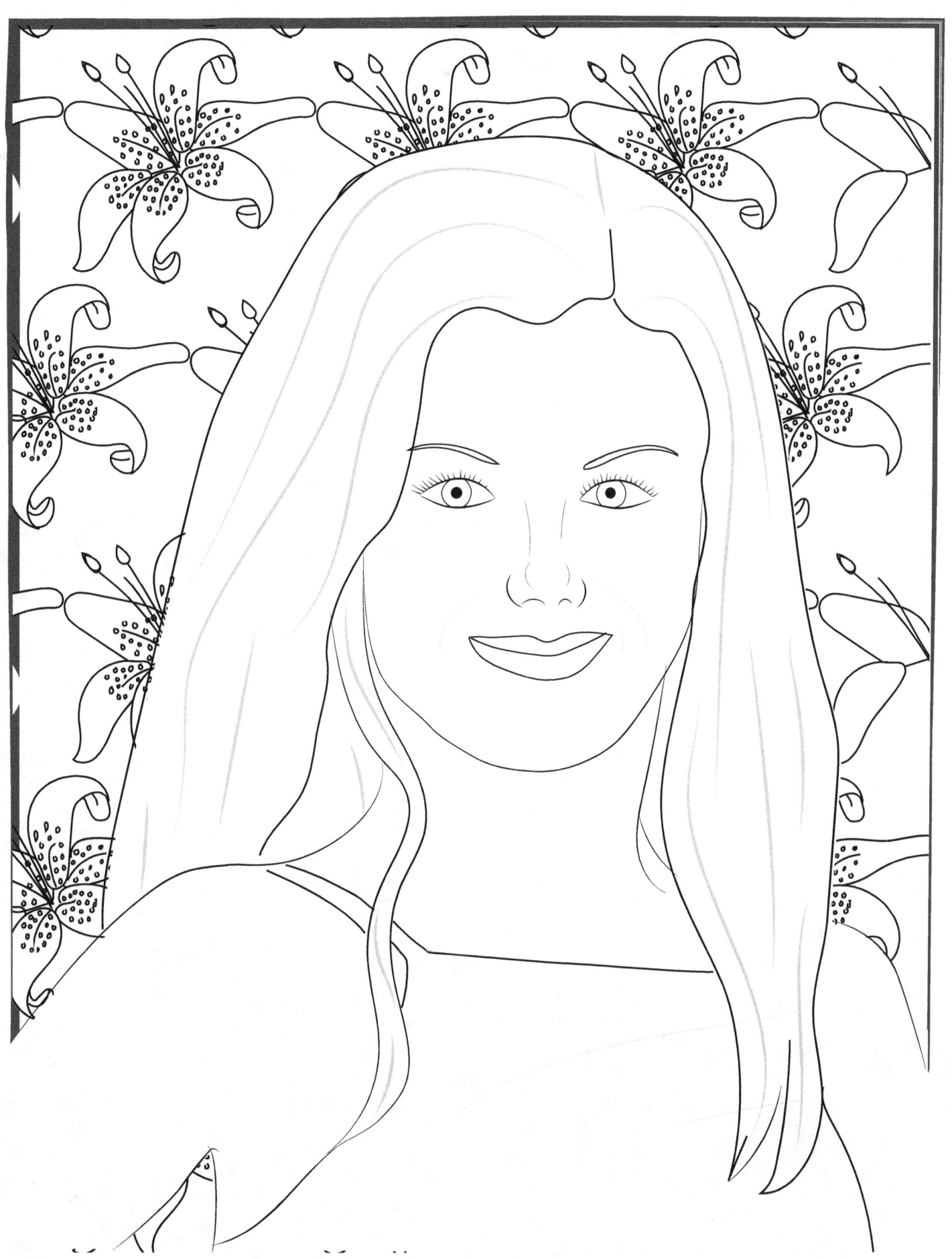

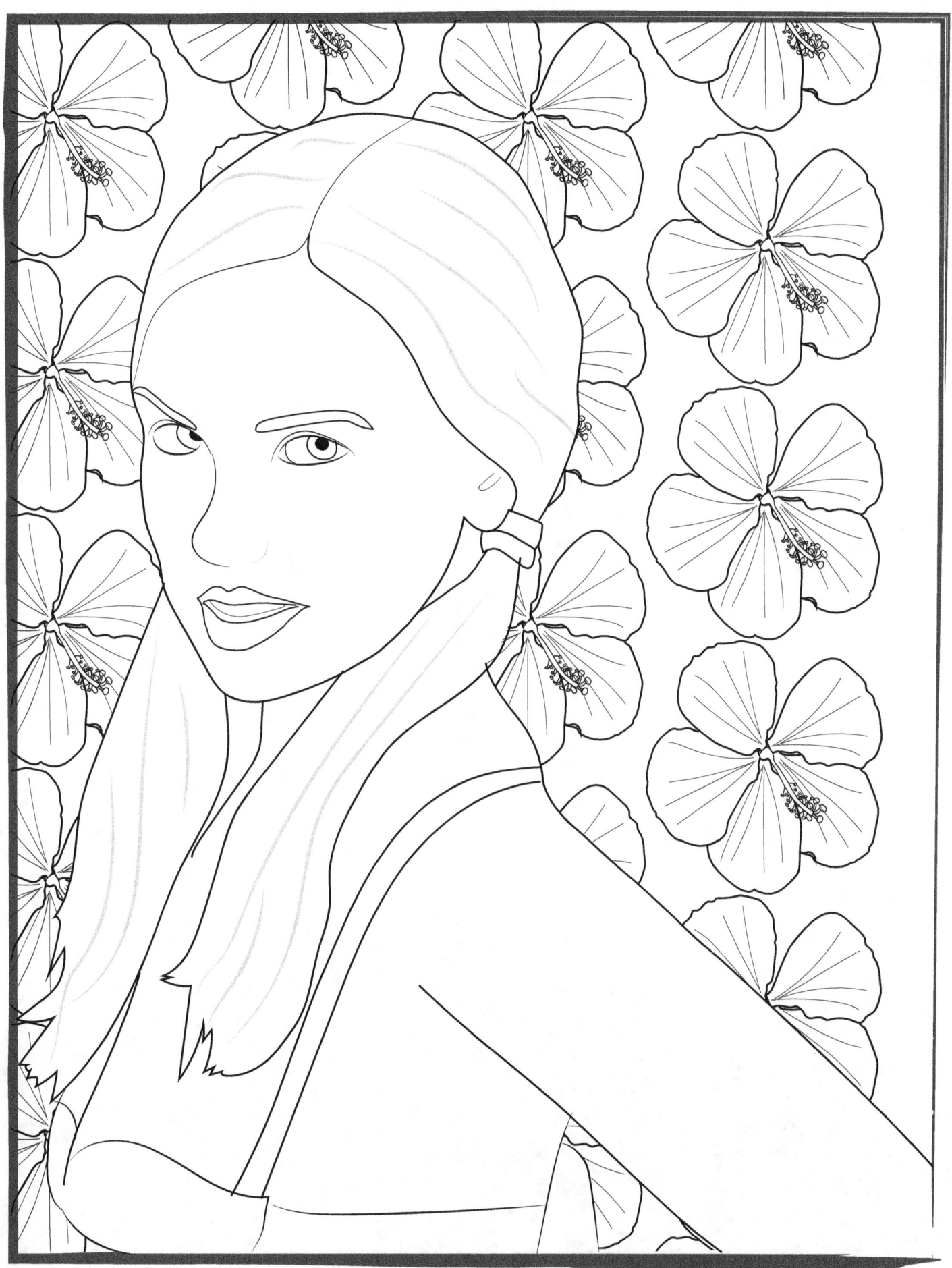

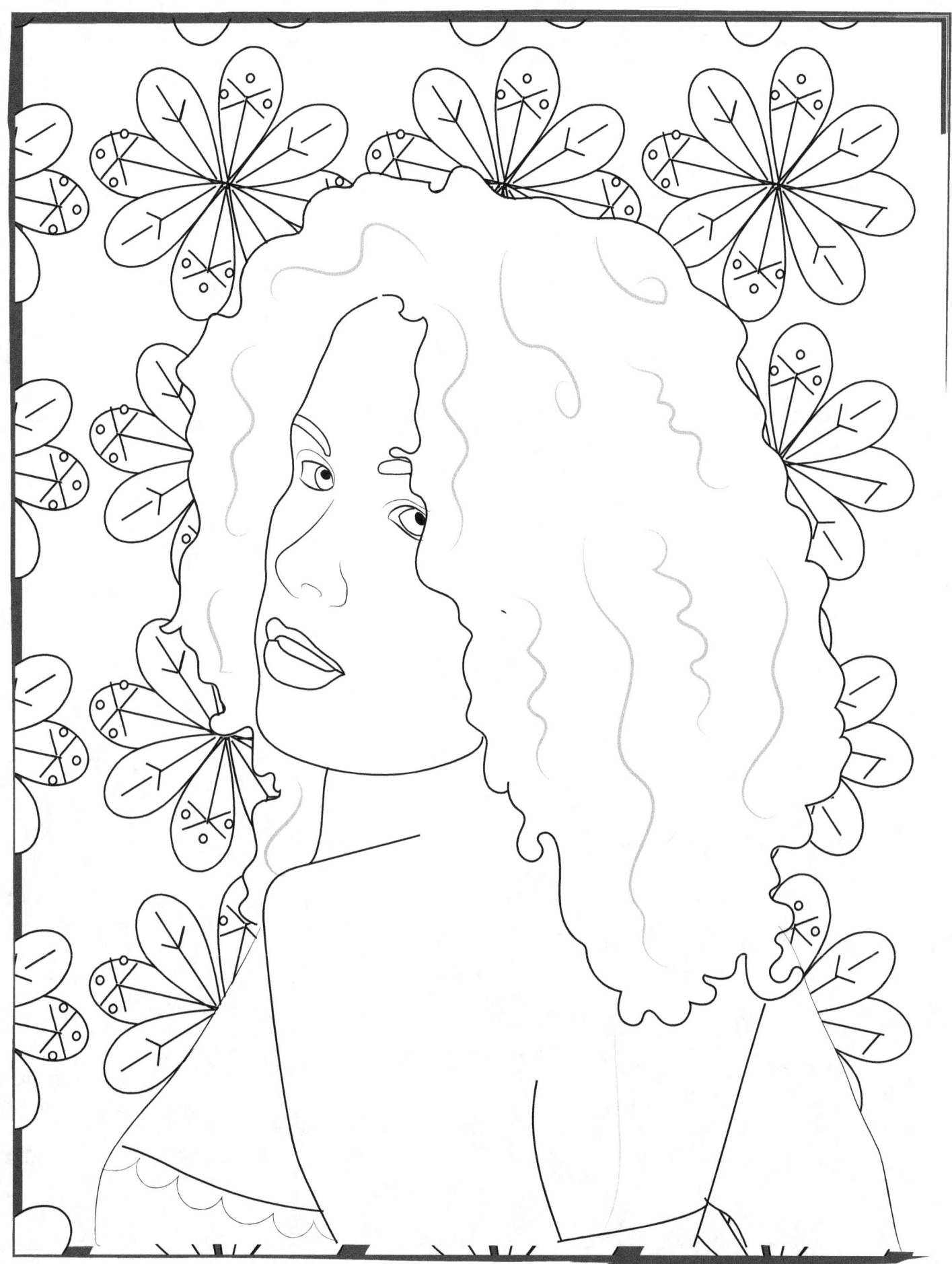

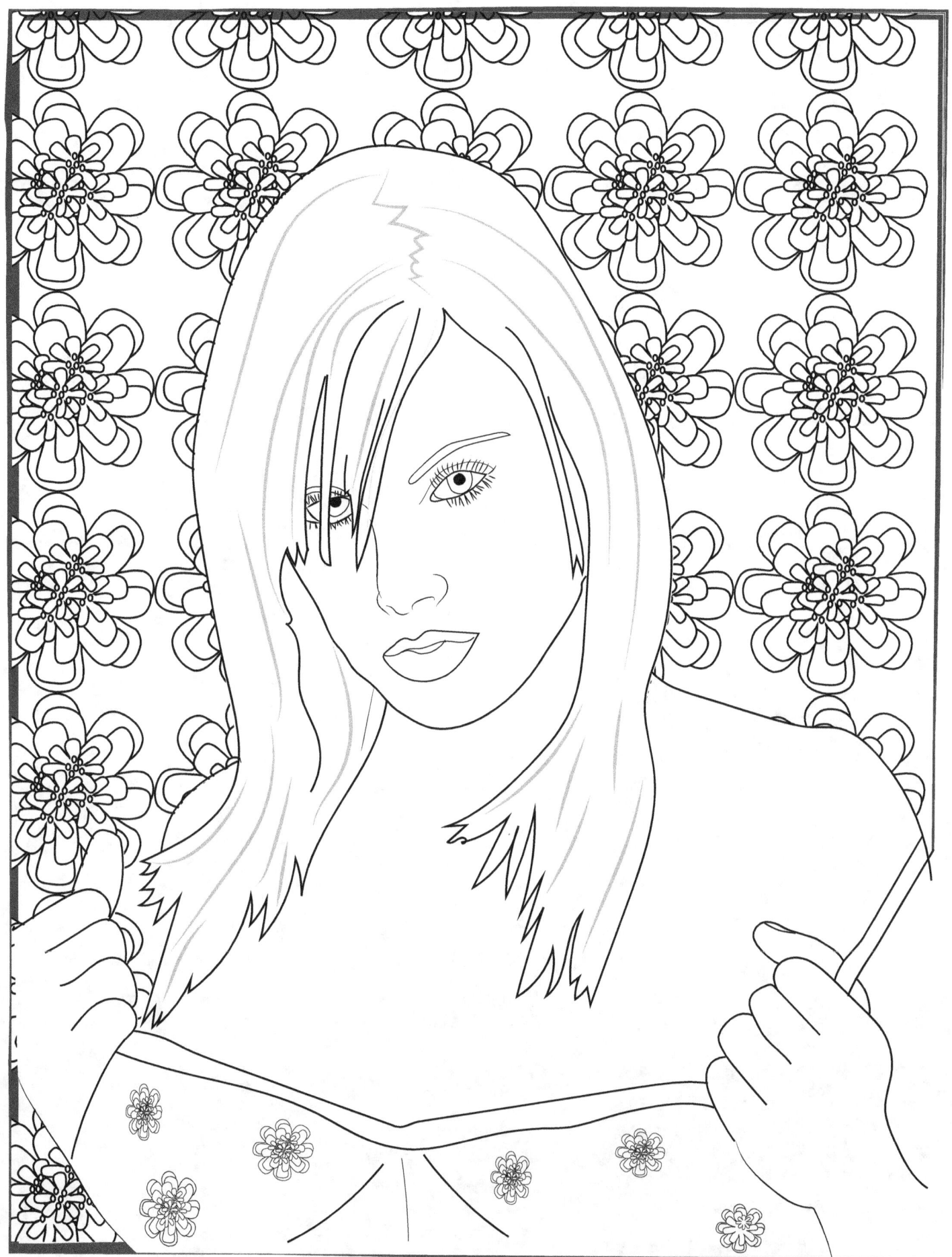

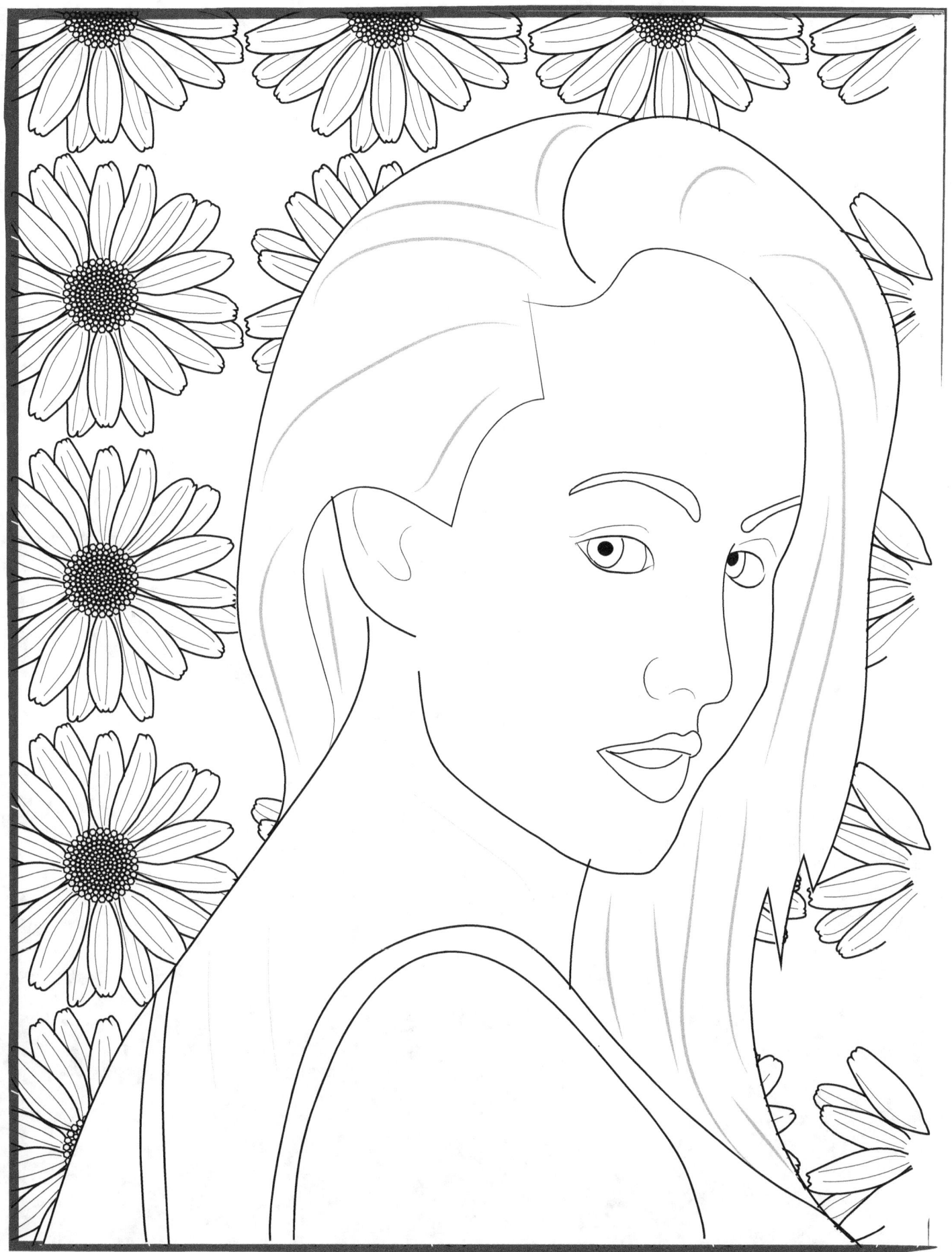

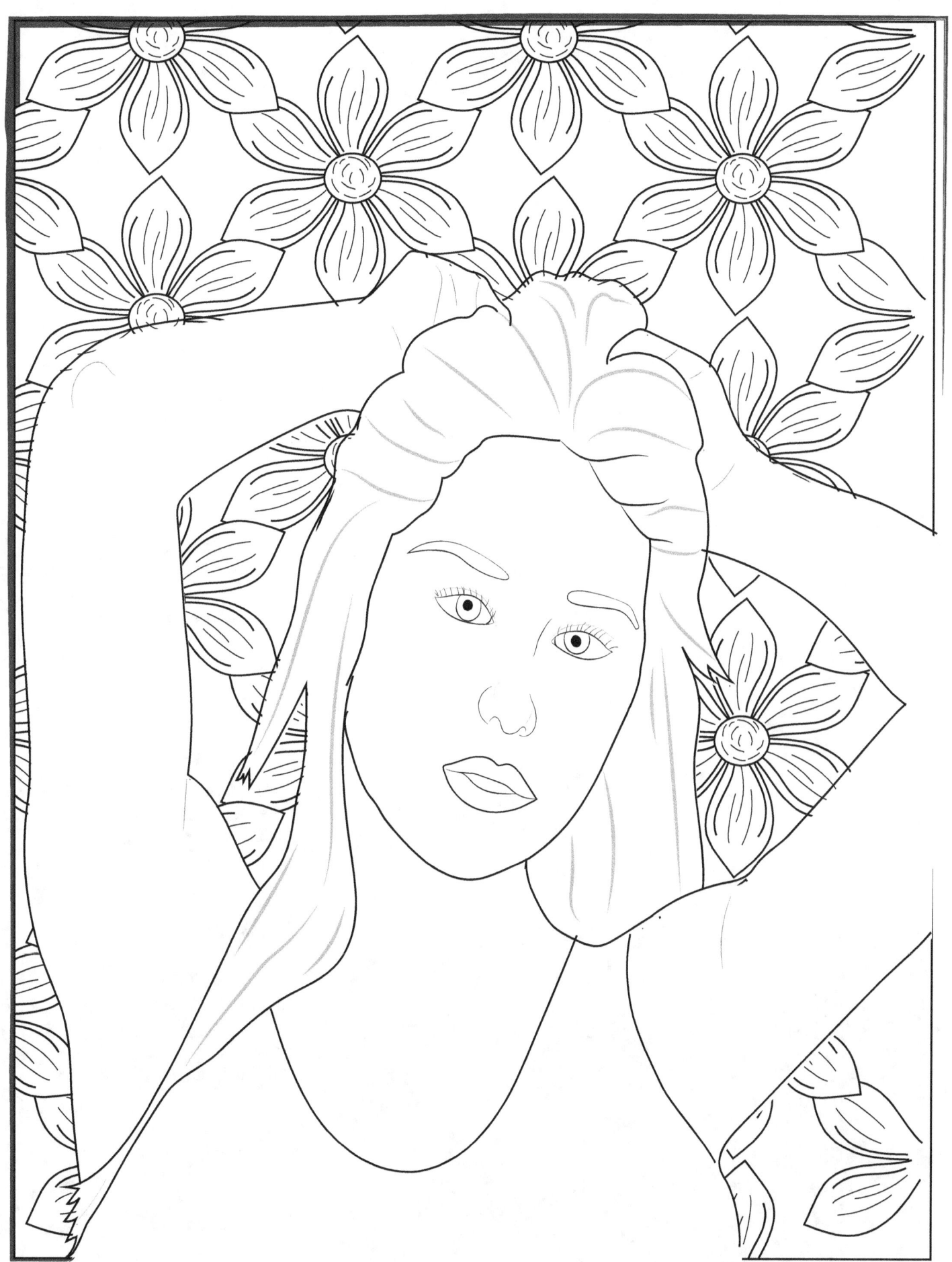

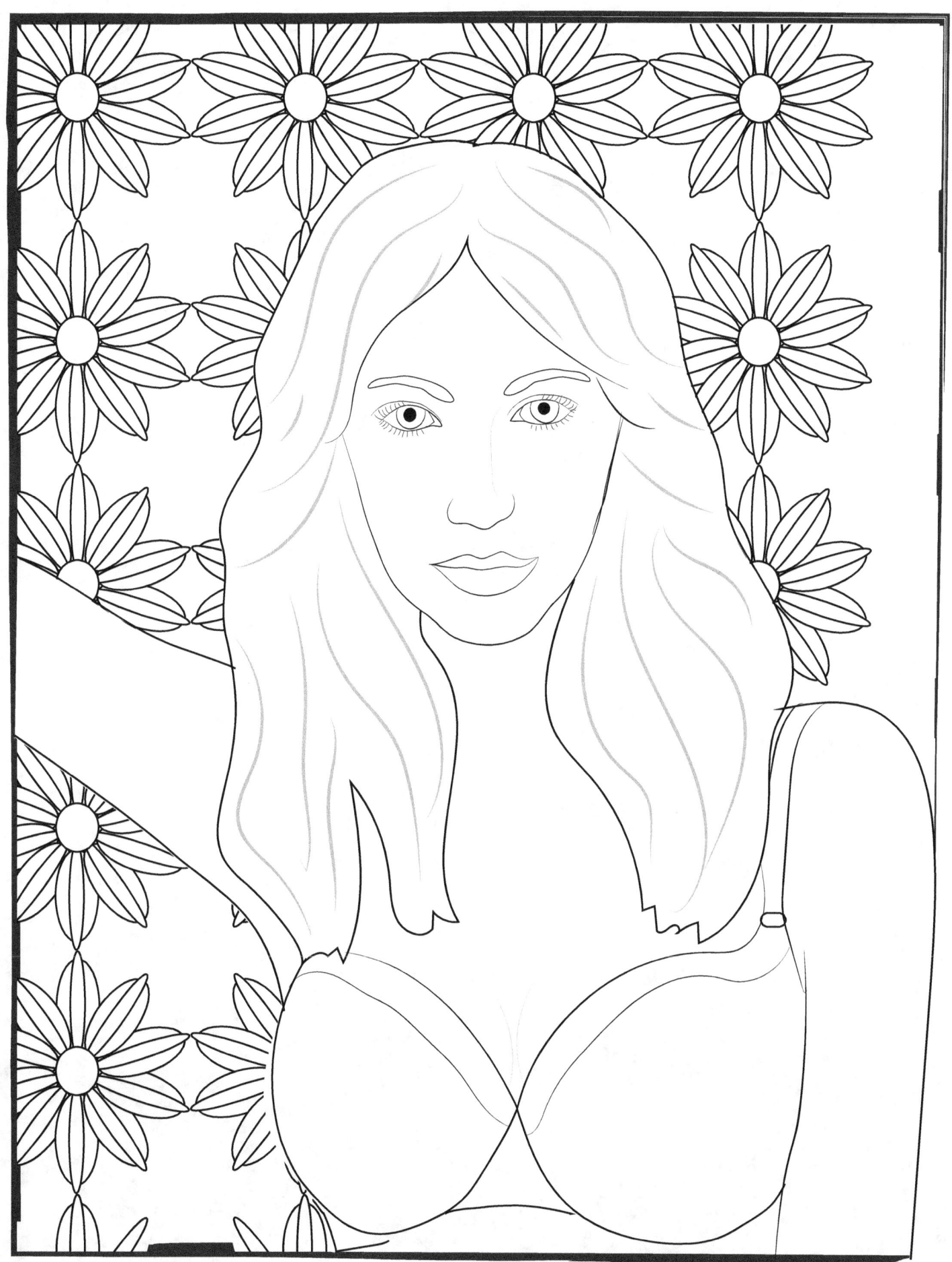

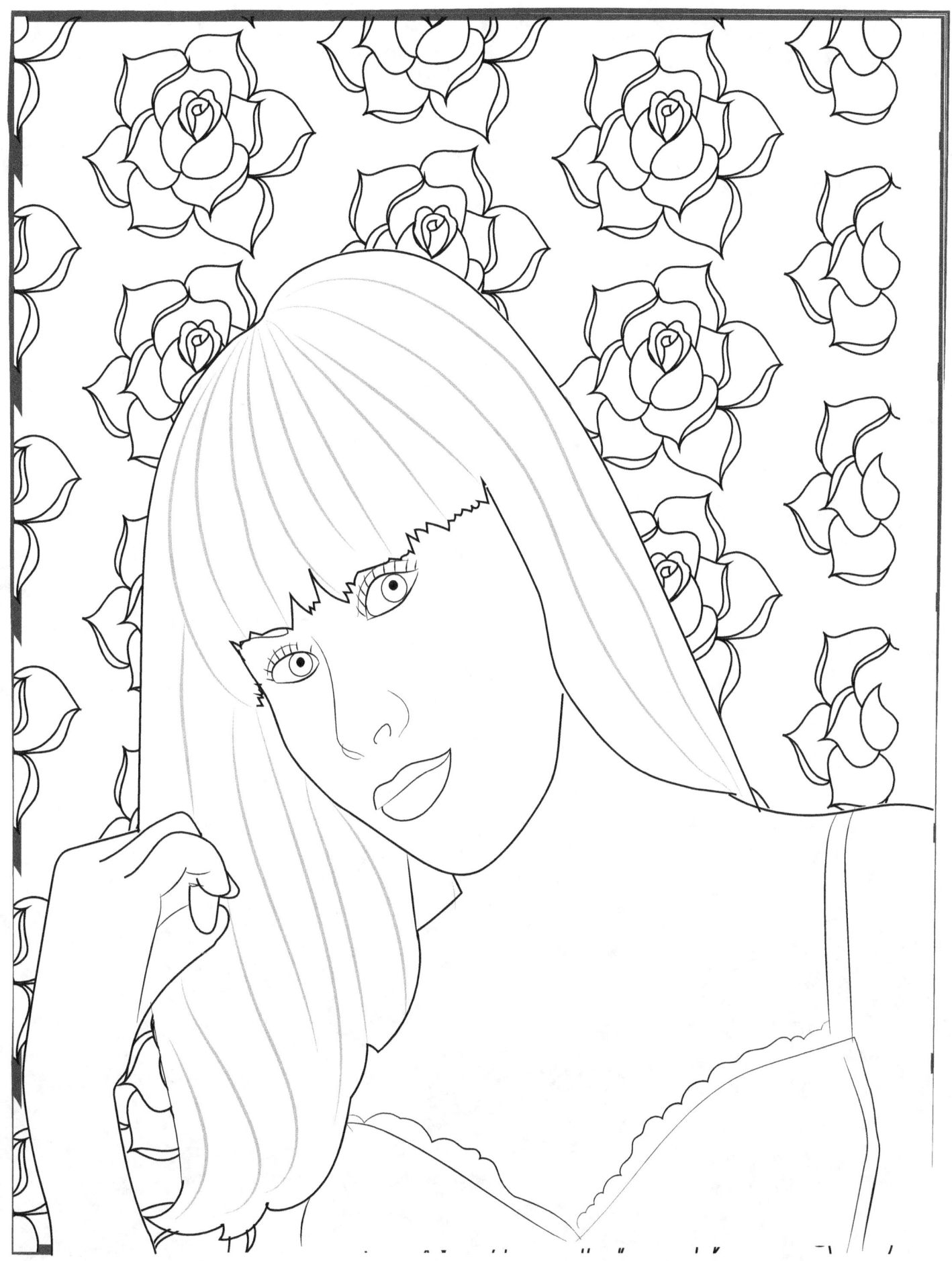

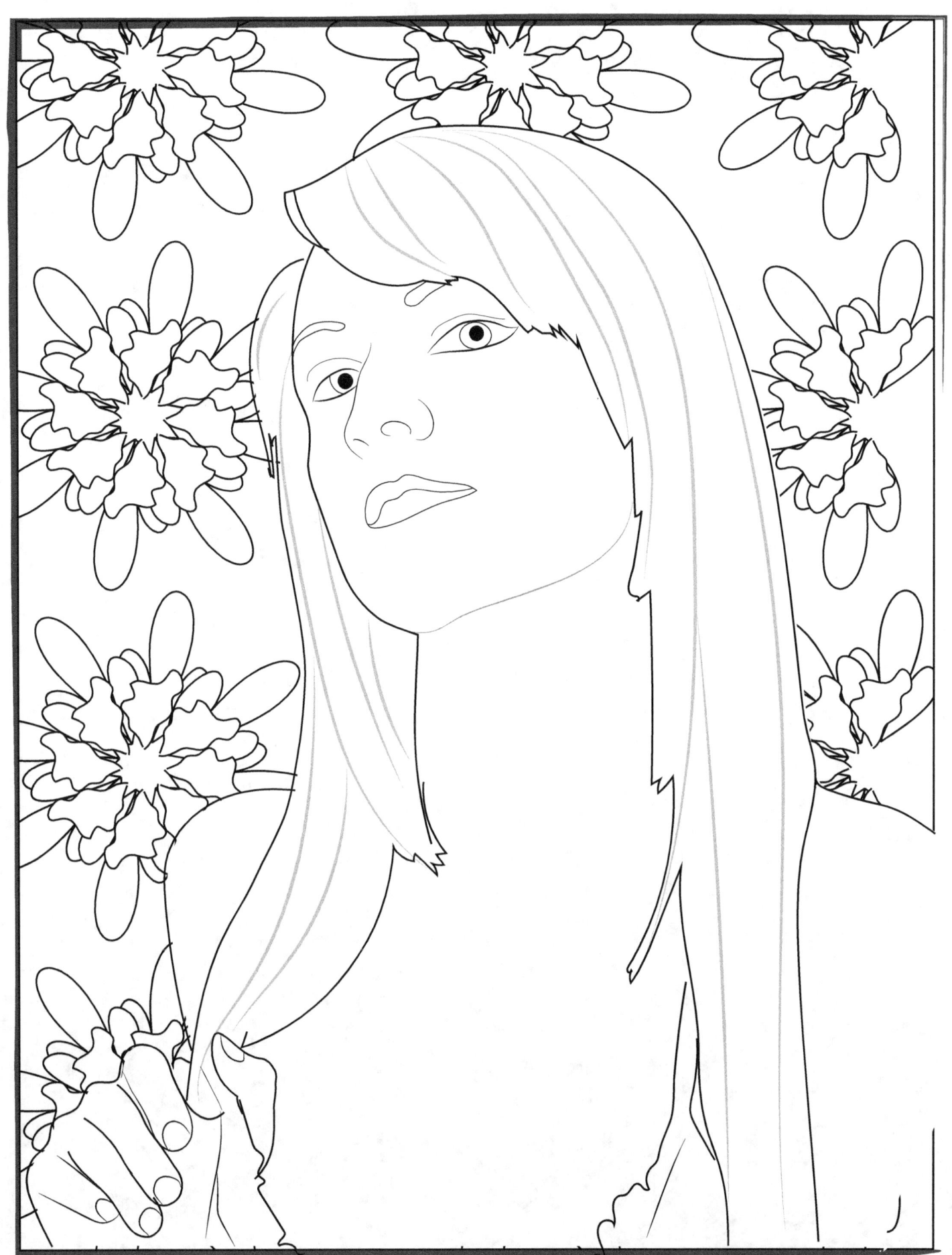

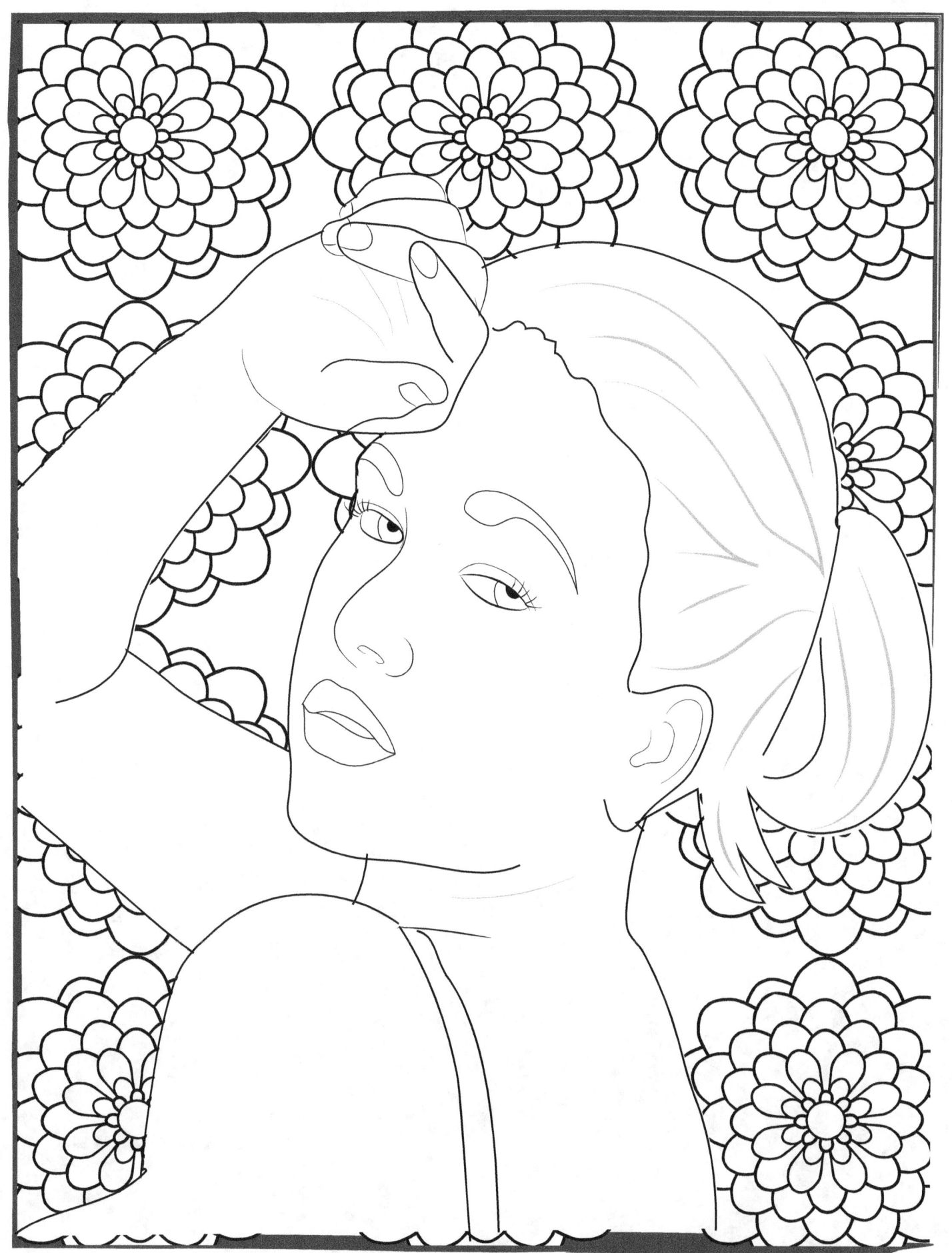

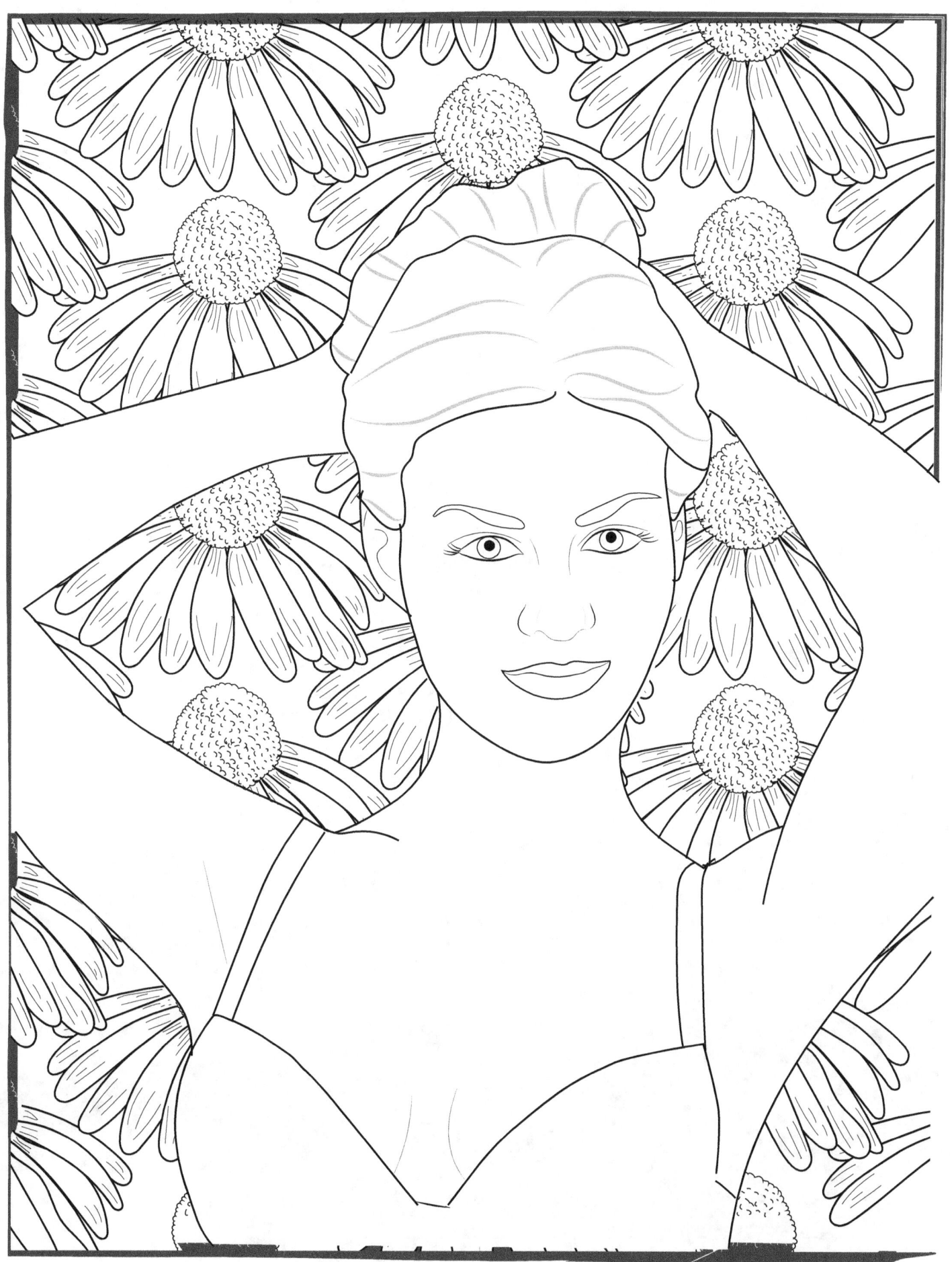

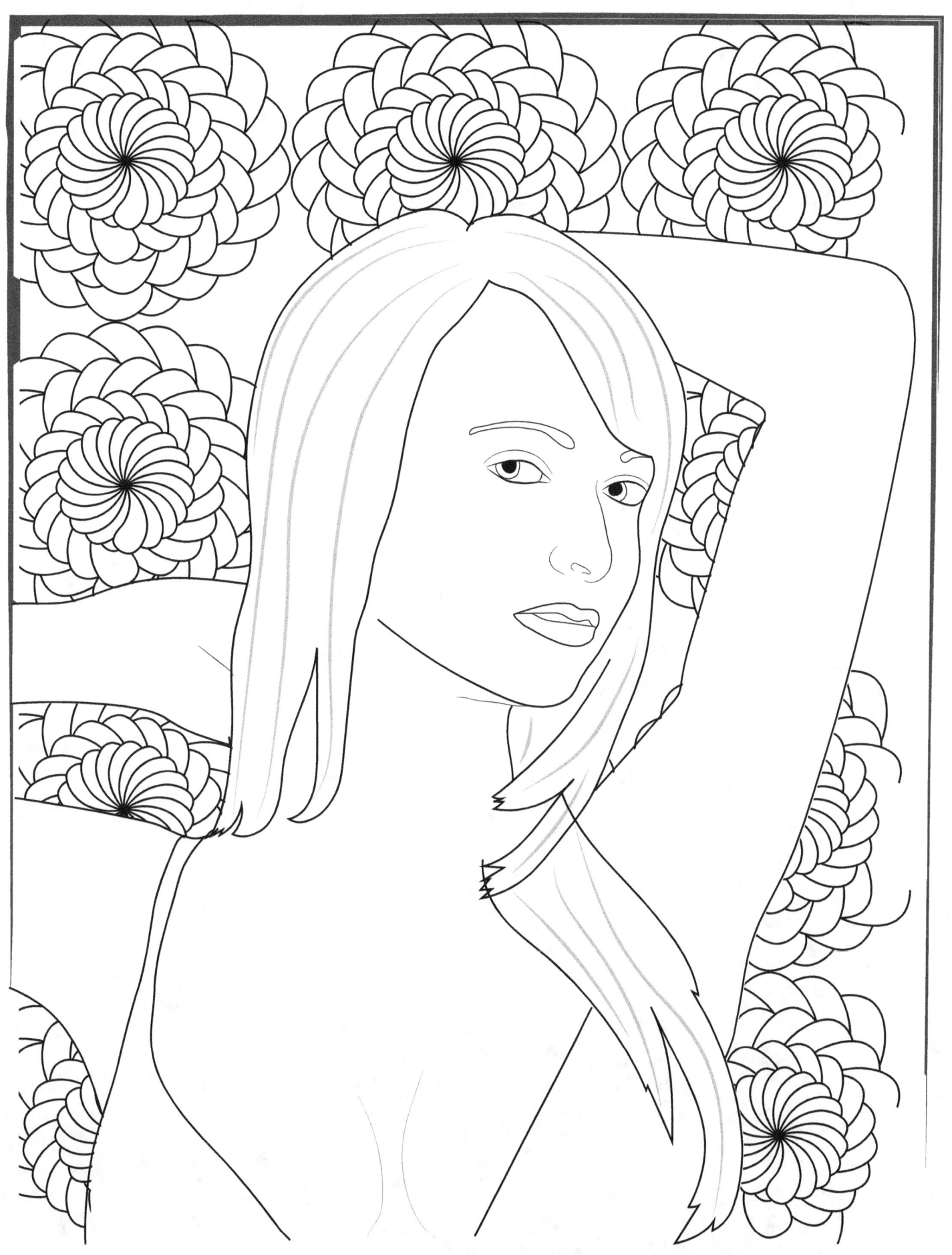

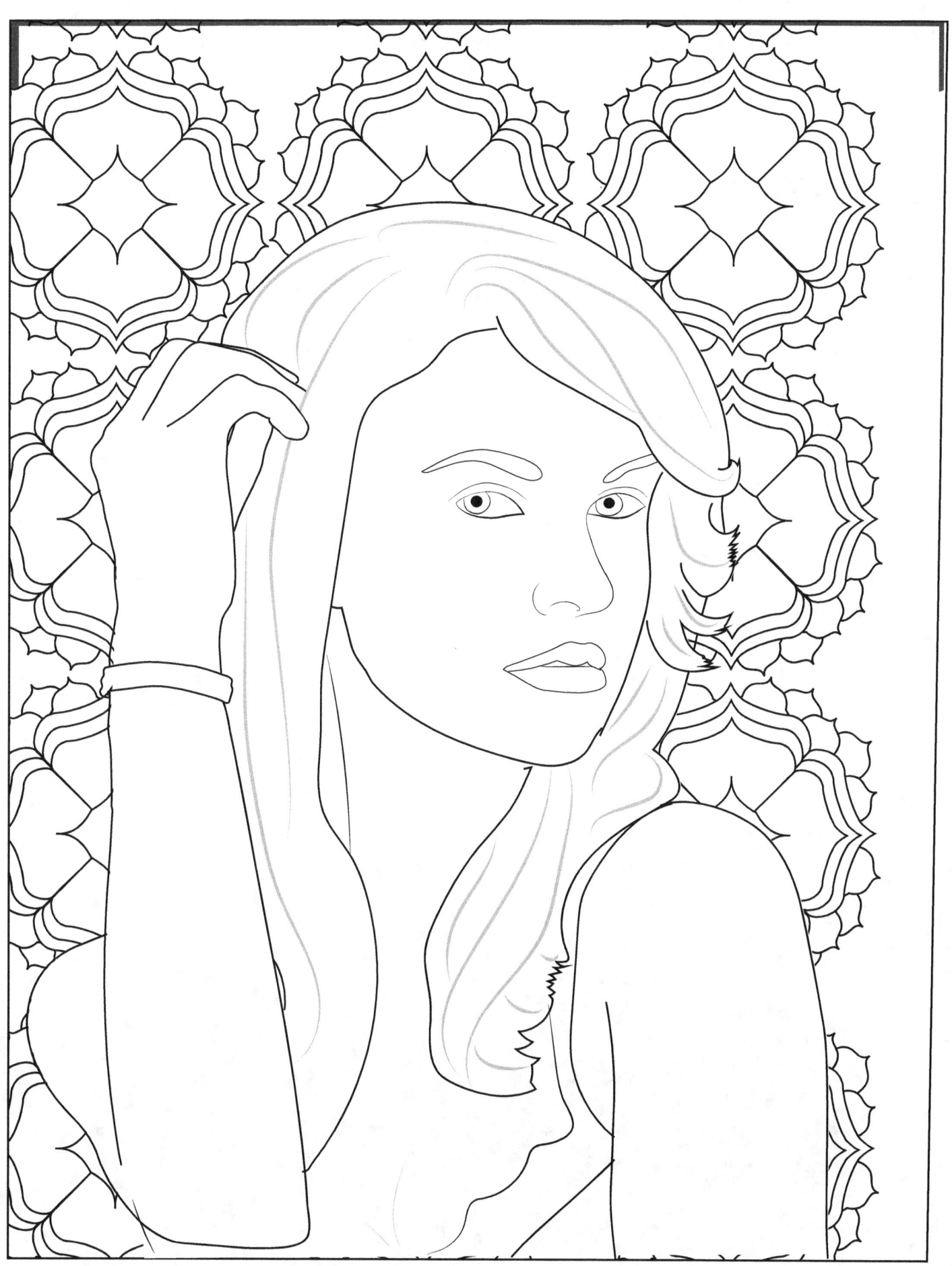

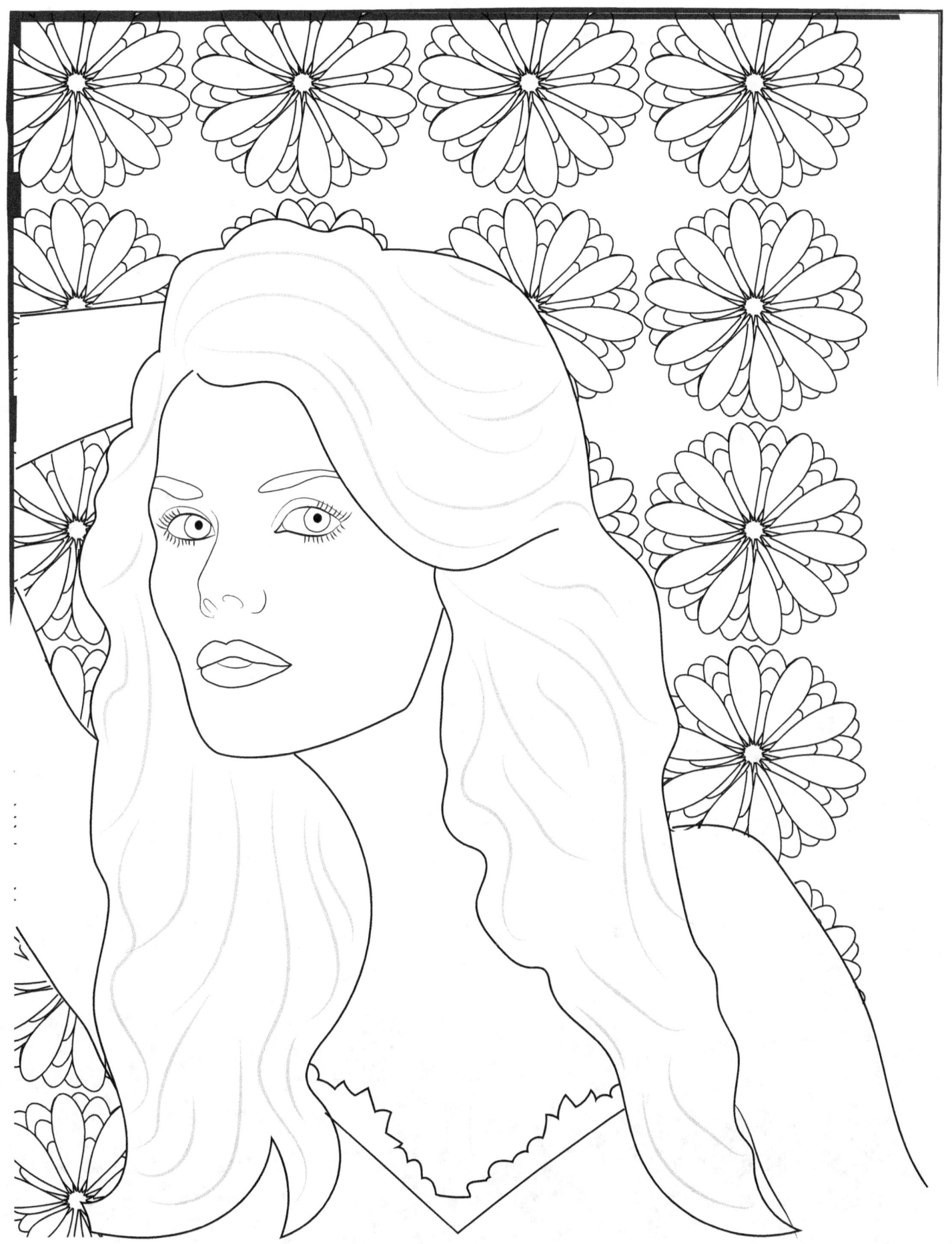

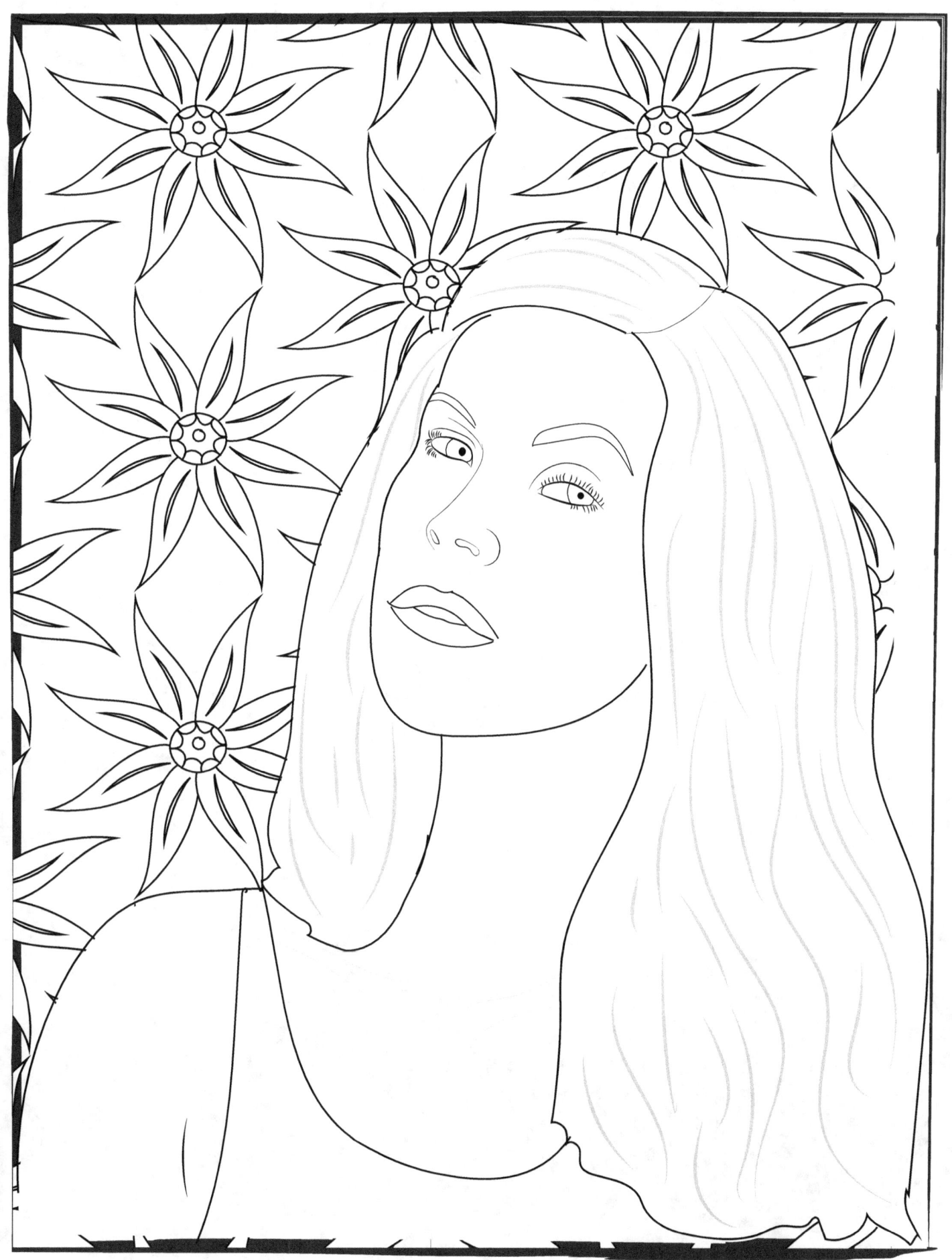

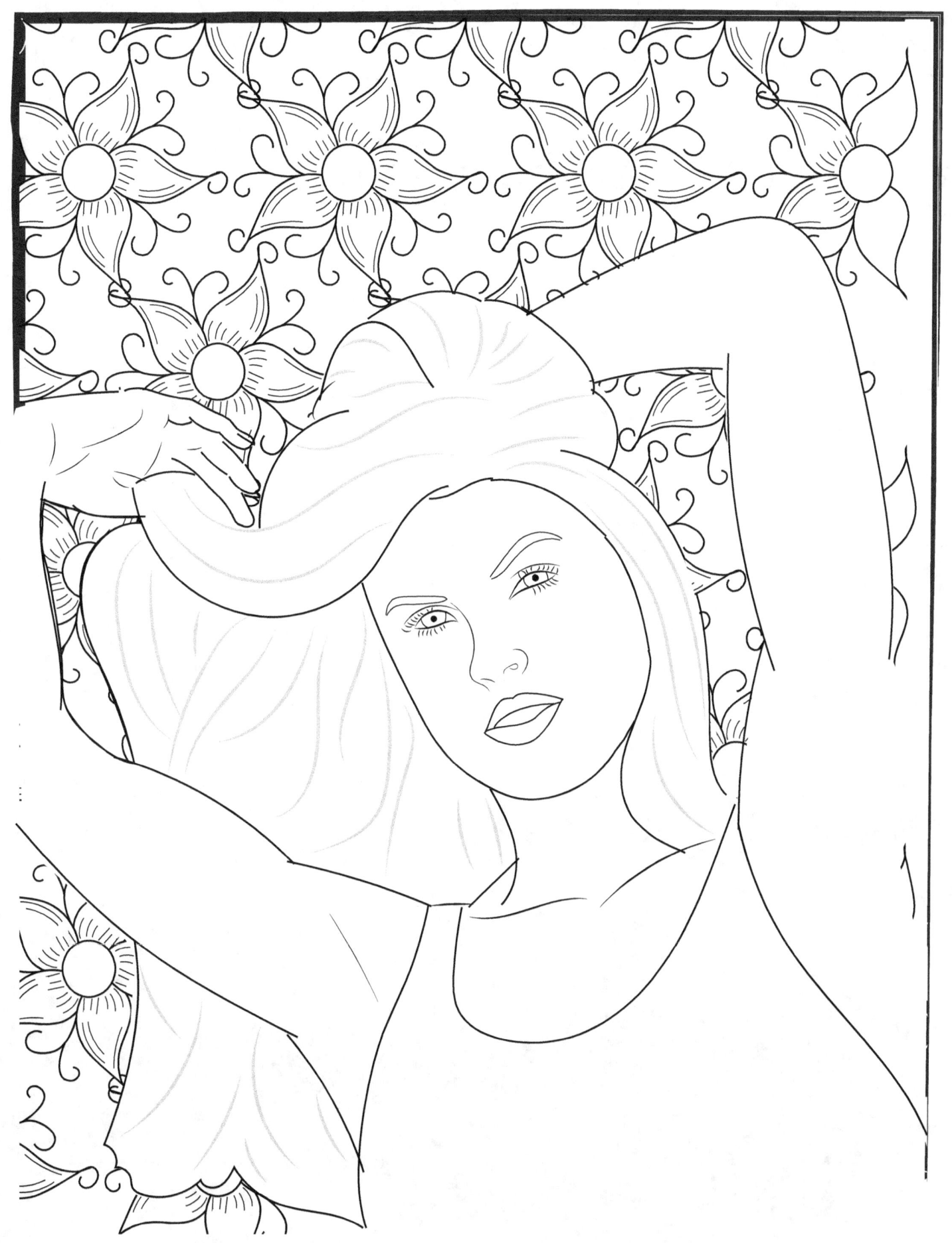

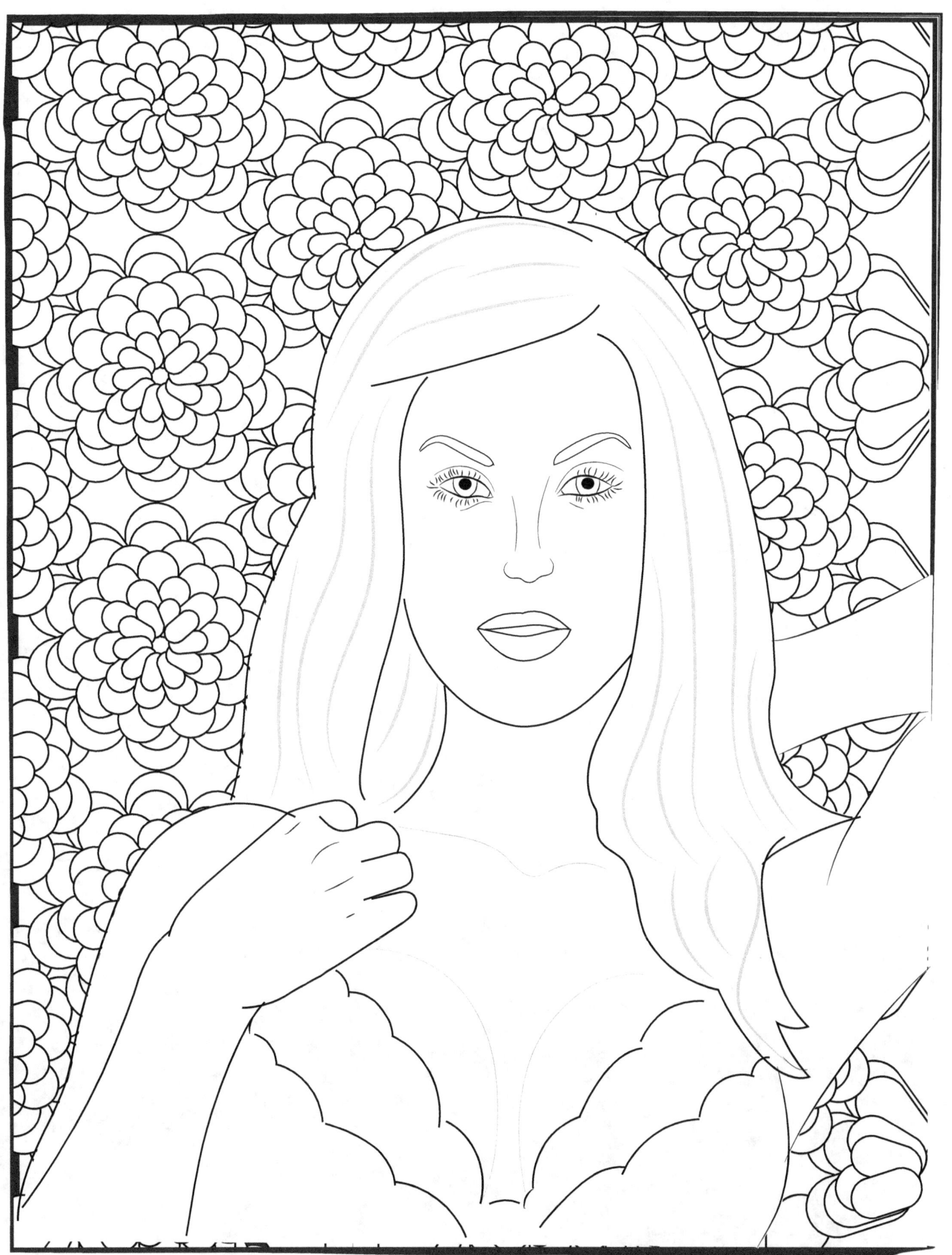

www.ingramcontent.com/pod-product-compliance
Lightning Source LLC
Chambersburg PA
CBHW081623220526
45468CB00010B/2998